I0782481

MYSTICAL BUSINESS SALE

Discover the skill of influence, next-level sales strategy, and hitting your stride in success.

By

Tiana C. Pels

TABLE OF CONTENTS

Are you ready to create magic

I hope you enjoy exploring the fascinating world of business magic! Be ready for an unparalleled spectacle that will captivate you with its brilliant demonstration of humor, wisdom, and whimsy. Let's take a fantastical journey where spreadsheets and wizardry meet before delving into the mysterious depths of next-level strategy.

Imagine a world in which PowerPoint presentations are magically interactive, CEOs don wizard hats, and boardrooms are converted into alchemical laboratories. The conference room table becomes a platform for breathtaking illusions, and the common office stapler transforms into a magical wand in this world. My friend, we are about to set out on an incredible journey where magic meets business, numbers come to life, and success is combined with a flick of the wrist.

You might be wondering, what exactly is this thing called business magic? Is it some sort of secret sorcery that effortlessly conjures up money? Or maybe it's the amazing ability to make piles of boring paperwork disappear in a flash? Well, my friend, it's all that and so much more. Business magic is like a hidden superpower that turns ordinary companies into unstoppable forces. It's like having a spell that mesmerizes customers, grabs the attention of investors, and makes your competition practically invisible!

Imagine this: with business magic, you can captivate people's attention and make them fall in love with your products or services. It's like casting a spell that makes customers flock to your business, eager to experience the magic you have to offer. And when it comes to investors, business magic is like a charm that entices them to open their wallets and support your ventures. They'll be so impressed by the enchanting aura you create that they won't be able to resist getting on board.

But that's not all. Business magic also gives you the power to outshine your competition. It's like having an invisibility cloak that makes your rivals fade into the background while you take the spotlight. With your magical strategies and innovative ideas, you'll leave them scratching their heads, wondering how you managed to stay steps ahead.

Get ready for an entertaining book that will uncover the mysteries of advanced strategies. We'll guide you through the fascinating world of enchanting marketing campaigns, clever negotiation techniques, and captivating leadership approaches. You'll discover the secrets to creating a company culture that feels like stepping into a magical wonderland, where everyone is inspired and motivated to do their best.

Imagine having the ability to charm your customers with mesmerizing marketing campaigns that leave them spellbound. You'll learn the tricks to create advertisements and promotions that grab attention and make people excited about your products or services. It's like casting a spell that makes customers fall under your business's enchanting spell.

But that's not all. We'll also delve into the realm of bewitching negotiation methods. You'll discover how to navigate tricky business deals with finesse and skill.

These techniques will empower you to sway negotiations in your favor, leaving your counterparts mesmerized and eager to reach a mutually beneficial agreement.

And when it comes to leadership, we'll show you how to create a workplace that feels like a magical wonderland. We'll explore strategies for fostering a positive and engaging company culture, where employees feel valued and motivated. It's like creating an atmosphere of excitement and wonder, where everyone is inspired to unleash their full potential.

So get ready to dive into the pages of this entertaining book. Through amusing anecdotes and practical advice, we'll unlock the secrets of next-level strategy, transforming your business into a realm of enchantment and success.

So, my friend, embrace the wonders of business magic.

It's not just about making money or getting rid of paperwork. It's an extraordinary force that can transform your business into something truly remarkable.

But before we delve into the nitty-gritty of business sorcery, we must lay the groundwork.

Just as a magician meticulously prepares before their grand performance, you must understand the importance of strategy "launching into action". In this introductory section, we will explore the foundations upon which business magic is built. From cultivating a magician's mindset to harnessing the powers of anticipation and foresight, we will equip you with the tools you need to conjure success from the very beginning.

So, fasten your seatbelts, grab your magic wand (or pen, if you prefer), and get ready for an exhilarating journey through the realms of business magic! Whether you're a seasoned sorcerer or a fledgling apprentice, this book is your ticket to unlocking the secrets of next-level strategy and achieving the extraordinary.

Remember, dear reader, in the world of business magic, the only limit is your imagination. So, let the adventure begin!

Introduction: Launching into Action

In the fast-paced and ever-evolving realm of business, success is not merely a result of luck or happenstance. It is the culmination of strategic thinking, innovative approaches, and a deep understanding of market dynamics. However, beyond these tangible elements lies an intangible force that sets exceptional entrepreneurs and leaders apart from the rest: their ability to harness the power of business magic. Just as a sorcerer wields their magic to shape the world around them, entrepreneurs and leaders possess a unique set of skills and mindsets that enable them to create their success. This chapter delves into the captivating world of business magic, where creativity, imagination, positivity, and belief converge to propel individuals toward whimsical success.

Unveiling the Secrets of Next-Level Strategy

In the competitive landscape of business, the need for effective strategies cannot be overstated. While traditional approaches and conventional thinking may yield moderate results, it is the infusion of magic into strategic decision-making that can truly unlock extraordinary outcomes. By understanding and utilizing the secrets of next-level strategy, entrepreneurs and leaders can transcend the boundaries of what is considered possible and set new standards of success. This chapter serves as a guide to unraveling the hidden secrets of next-level strategy. It explores how visionary leaders leverage their creative thinking, adaptability, and deep understanding of market dynamics to craft innovative strategies that defy expectations. From disruptive business models to revolutionary product development, the secrets revealed here will empower individuals to navigate the complex business landscape with finesse and achieve remarkable results.

Setting the Stage for Whimsical Success

In the quest for success, something remarkable happens when people embrace a more imaginative and open-minded approach. They break away from their usual routines and traditional ways of thinking and instead embrace their imagination, the potential for new possibilities, and a strong belief in their abilities. This change in mindset creates the perfect conditions for what we call *"whimsical success,"* where extraordinary achievements become the norm. Within the confines of this chapter, we lay the groundwork for individuals to embark on a transformative journey toward whimsical success. We understand that true growth and extraordinary achievements lie beyond the boundaries of comfort and familiarity. Therefore, we implore individuals to take bold steps outside their comfort zones, daring to explore uncharted territories in their pursuit of success.

One of the key ingredients to unlocking whimsical success is the exploration of creativity. We encourage individuals to tap into their innate imaginative powers, allowing their minds to wander freely and uncover new and innovative ideas. By embracing their creativity, they can break the shackles of conventional thinking and discover unique approaches that can propel them toward extraordinary accomplishments.

Moreover, a positive outlook plays a pivotal role in the journey towards whimsical success. It is through cultivating a mindset of optimism and resilience that individuals can overcome obstacles and setbacks that inevitably arise along the way. By maintaining a positive perspective, they can find hidden opportunities amidst challenges and bounce back stronger than ever before. By venturing into the realm of whimsical success, individuals have the opportunity to unlock their full potential.

This entails recognizing and harnessing their unique strengths, talents, and abilities. With self-belief and confidence, they can push the boundaries of what they thought was possible, surpassing their expectations and reaching new heights of achievement.

Ultimately, this chapter serves as a guide for individuals to embark on a journey filled with imagination, creativity, and positivity. It empowers them to break free from the confines of routine and conventional thinking, paving the way for remarkable accomplishments and whimsical success.
As we venture further into the realms of business magic, let us unlock the secrets of next-level strategy and set the stage for whimsical success. Prepare to embark on a transformative journey that will empower you to wield the forces of creativity, imagination, positivity, and belief, and shape your entrepreneurial destiny like a true business sorcerer.

Chapter1:The Mindset of a Business Sorcerer

In the business world, achieving success is frequently linked to being innovative, adaptable, and having a deep comprehension of market trends. Nevertheless, there is a mysterious aspect that distinguishes exceptional entrepreneurs and leaders from others, and that is their mindset. This section explores the mindset of a business sorcerer, an individual who harnesses the power of creativity, imagination, positivity, and belief to shape their path as an entrepreneur.

Success in the business world often comes hand in hand with being innovative, adaptable, and having a keen understanding of market dynamics. However, what sets exceptional entrepreneurs and leaders apart is their mindset, which cannot be measured concretely. This chapter explores the mindset of a business sorcerer, an individual who possesses the remarkable power to wield creativity, imagination, positivity, and strong belief to shape their journey as an entrepreneur.

Embracing creativity and imagination

The realm of business is not solely governed by logic and rationality. It is the infusion of creativity and imagination that sets exceptional entrepreneurs apart from the rest. These business sorcerers possess a deep appreciation for the power of these qualities, recognizing that they serve as catalysts for innovation and transformation.

Creativity is the spark that ignites the entrepreneurial fire. It is the ability to think beyond the ordinary, to see possibilities where

---

[1] Mystical business sales

others see limitations. Business sorcerers understand that the greatest breakthroughs often emerge from uncharted territories, where they dare to venture into unexplored realms of ideas and concepts. By fostering a creative mindset, they uncover unique perspectives and solutions that disrupt industries and captivate audiences.

Imagination, on the other hand, is the canvas on which these entrepreneurs paint their visions. It is the realm of boundless possibilities where dreams take shape. Business sorcerers possess the remarkable ability to harness their imagination, conjuring up vivid images of what could be. They envision products and services that fill unmet needs, envision new business models that challenge the status quo, and conceive strategies that propel their ventures to new heights.

With creativity and imagination as their guiding forces, these business sorcerers challenge conventional wisdom. They question established norms and explore alternative paths.

They are unafraid to take risks and embrace uncertainty, knowing that it is through these leaps of faith that true innovation is born.

Moreover, creativity and imagination breathe life into the entrepreneurial journey. They infuse it with passion, inspiration, and a sense of wonder. Business sorcerers understand that by embracing these qualities, they can create a work environment that nurtures innovation and attracts like-minded individuals who share their vision.

In the realm of business sorcery, creativity, and imagination are not mere luxuries; they are essential tools for success. They enable entrepreneurs to forge new paths, disrupt industries, and leave an indelible mark on the world. By embracing these qualities, business sorcerers tap into their true powers, transforming the mundane into the extraordinary and shaping the future of business with their visionary magic.

To fully embrace and unleash the power of creativity and imagination, it is important to create an environment that supports and encourages these magical qualities. This can be done by fostering a space where ideas can be freely shared and explored. One way to achieve this is through brainstorming sessions, where everyone is encouraged to contribute their thoughts and ideas without judgment. By bringing together diverse perspectives and experiences, business sorcerers can tap into a wealth of creativity and uncover innovative solutions to even the most complex problems.

In addition, cultivating a culture that values experimentation and risk-taking is vital. This means embracing the idea that failure is not a setback but an opportunity for growth and learning. By encouraging business sorcerers to take calculated risks and try new approaches, they are empowered to push the boundaries of what is possible and discover groundbreaking ideas that can transform their ventures.

Cultivating a Positive and Playful Attitude

Developing a positive and playful attitude is crucial for anyone adopting the business sorcerer mindset. When you embark on an entrepreneurial journey, you will face numerous challenges, setbacks, and uncertainties. Imagine starting your own business and encountering difficulties like limited funds, fierce competition, or unexpected obstacles.

In such situations, having a positive mindset is like having a superpower. It helps you stay resilient and grow despite the difficulties. For example, let's say you face a setback where a major client cancels a deal. Instead of getting discouraged or giving up a positive attitude enables you to see it as an opportunity for growth. You might think, "Okay, this door closed, but maybe there's another even better opportunity waiting for me."

Having a playful attitude is equally important. It means not taking everything too seriously and finding joy in the process. For instance, you might encounter a problem that seems insurmountable. Instead of getting overwhelmed, a playful mindset allows you to approach it creatively and experiment with different solutions. You might think, "Let's have some fun with this challenge and see if we can come up with an innovative solution that no one else has thought of."

Overall, cultivating a positive and playful attitude in the face of obstacles helps you stay motivated, bounce back from setbacks, and discover new possibilities. It allows you to approach problems with a fresh perspective, adapt to changes, and ultimately

thrive in the unpredictable world of entrepreneurship. Maintaining a positive attitude involves reframing setbacks as opportunities for learning and personal development. Instead of being discouraged by failures, business sorcerers view them as stepping stones on the path to success. They understand that setbacks provide valuable lessons and insights that can propel them forward.

For example, let's say a business sorcerer launches a new product that doesn't perform as expected in the market. Rather than dwelling on the disappointment, they analyze the situation, identify the reasons for the product's failure, and use that knowledge to improve future offerings. They might realize that they need to refine their marketing strategy, conduct more thorough market research, or enhance the product's features based on customer feedback. By adopting this positive mindset, they transform setbacks into opportunities for growth and development.

In addition to reframing setbacks, business sorcerers approach challenges with curiosity and a sense of playfulness. They recognize that a playful mindset can spark creativity and open doors to innovative solutions. For instance, imagine a business sorcerer faces the logistical challenge of delivering their products to customers within a tight timeframe. Instead of becoming overwhelmed by the problem, they approach it with a playful attitude. They might brainstorm unusual ideas, such as using drones for deliveries, partnering with local businesses for distribution, or organizing a fun event where customers can pick up their orders. By embracing playfulness, they tap into their imagination and explore unconventional approaches that can lead to breakthrough solutions.

Moreover, maintaining a positive and playful attitude enables business sorcerers to venture into uncharted territories. They are not afraid of taking risks or stepping outside their comfort zones because they see these endeavors as opportunities for growth and expansion.

For example, a business sorcerer might decide to explore a new market segment or introduce a completely different product line. Instead of being limited by fear or uncertainty, they approach these ventures with excitement and a sense of adventure. They are willing to embrace the unknown, learn from their experiences, and adapt their strategies along the way.

This willingness to explore new frontiers can lead to remarkable discoveries and unexpected successes. Note that, a positive mindset is infectious and can inspire and motivate teams. When leaders exude positivity, it creates an environment where creativity and collaboration thrive, leading to higher employee engagement and productivity.

In summary, maintaining a positive attitude involves reframing setbacks as learning opportunities, approaching challenges with curiosity and playfulness, and embracing the unknown. By adopting this mindset, business sorcerers can turn failures into stepping stones, find innovative solutions through playful exploration, and venture into uncharted territories with confidence.

Harnessing the power of belief and confidence

Having faith in oneself and the business vision is a key part of the business sorcerer mindset. A Business sorcerer strongly believes in their skills and has the unwavering conviction that they can overcome any challenge that comes their way. This unwavering belief gives them the determination, perseverance, and resilience needed to navigate through tough times and keep pushing forward.

Imagine a business sorcerer starting their own company. They have a clear vision of what they want to achieve and believe in their abilities to make it happen. Even when faced with obstacles like financial difficulties or fierce competition, they don't lose hope. They know that with their skills, knowledge, and hard work, they can find a way to overcome these challenges and succeed.

This belief in oneself and the business vision acts as a driving force. It keeps the business sorcerer motivated and focused on their goals. It helps them stay committed even when things get tough and setbacks occur.

Instead of giving up, they use these challenges as opportunities to grow and improve. For example, let's say a business sorcerer launches a new product that doesn't initially gain much traction in the market. Instead of doubting themselves or losing confidence, they see it as a chance to learn and adapt. They analyze customer feedback, make adjustments to the product, and refine their marketing strategies. Their belief in themselves and their vision gives them the confidence to persevere and find a way to turn things around.

In summary, the business sorcerer mindset includes a strong belief in oneself and the business vision. This belief provides the motivation, determination, and resilience needed to overcome obstacles and achieve success. It keeps the business sorcerer focused, committed, and open to learning from setbacks. With this unwavering belief, they can face challenges head-on and continue working towards their goals.

To harness the power of belief and confidence, it is essential to cultivate self-awareness and develop a strong sense of purpose. Understanding one's strengths, weaknesses, and values enables business sorcerers to align their actions with their vision and make decisions that are congruent with their goals.

Additionally, surrounding oneself with a supportive network of mentors, advisors, and like-minded individuals can bolster belief and confidence. The power of positive influence and encouragement cannot be underestimated, as it provides a source of motivation and accountability.

Business sorcerers also recognize the importance of continuous learning and personal growth. They invest in their development, seeking out opportunities to expand their knowledge, acquire new skills, and stay ahead of industry trends. This commitment to growth not only enhances expertise but also reinforces belief in their ability to adapt and succeed in a rapidly evolving business landscape.In conclusion, the mindset of a business sorcerer is characterized by embracing creativity and imagination, cultivating a positive and playful attitude, and harnessing the power of belief and confidence.

Chapter 2: The Spell-book of Marketing

In the realm of business sorcery, marketing is a potent tool that can weave spells of attraction, captivate audiences, and create lasting connections with customers. This chapter explores the essential elements found within the spellbook of marketing magic, including crafting captivating campaigns, conjuring compelling brand storytelling, and enchanting customers with magical experiences.

Crafting Captivating Campaigns

Captivating campaigns act like powerful spells that grab the target audience's attention and motivate them to take action. Creating such campaigns requires business sorcerers to have a deep understanding of their audience. This involves conducting comprehensive market research, identifying the needs, desires, and challenges of customers, and segmenting the audience to deliver tailored messages effectively.

Imagine a business sorcerer who wants to launch a new product. They know that to entice customers, they need to create a campaign that truly resonates with their target audience. To do this, they start by diving into thorough market research. They gather information about their potential customers, such as their demographics, preferences, and behaviors. This helps them gain insights into what motivates their audience and what problems they are seeking solutions for.

Armed with this knowledge, the business sorcerer can then identify the specific needs, desires, and pain points of their target audience. They understand the challenges their customers face and how their products can address those challenges effectively.

This understanding allows them to craft messages and campaigns that speak directly to their audience's concerns and aspirations. Segmenting the audience is another crucial step for business sorcerers. They divide their target market into smaller groups based on shared characteristics or behaviors. By doing so, they can create tailored messages that resonate with each segment. For example, if they have identified two distinct customer segments with different preferences, they can design separate campaigns to appeal to each group's specific needs and desires.

By closely studying their audience, conducting market research, identifying customer needs, desires, and pain points, and segmenting the audience effectively, business sorcerers can craft captivating campaigns that cast a spell on their target audience. These campaigns not only grab attention but also inspire action, ultimately leading to successful marketing outcomes and business growth.

The next step in the process is to generate a captivating and compelling narrative that truly resonates with the intended audience. This can be accomplished by crafting a well-structured story that revolves around the product or service being promoted. The story should highlight the unique value proposition of the offering and effectively communicate how it solves the customers' problems or enhances their lives.

To create an emotional connection with the audience, the marketing campaign should incorporate a mix of creative elements. These elements may include visually appealing graphics or videos that grab attention and leave a lasting impression.

Additionally, persuasive copywriting that effectively communicates the benefits and advantages of the product or service is crucial.

Engaging storytelling techniques can also be employed to captivate the audience. This may involve using relatable characters, anecdotes, or real-life examples that resonate with the target market. By weaving these storytelling elements into the campaign, it

becomes easier to establish a sense of empathy and emotional engagement with the audience.

Ultimately, the goal is to create a marketing campaign that not only informs customers about the product or service but also evokes a strong emotional response. By showcasing the unique value proposition and demonstrating how it addresses customer needs, the campaign becomes more memorable and persuasive.

 Additionally, it's important to use data and analytics to figure out how well marketing campaigns are working and make smart decisions based on that information. This means looking at important numbers and feedback from customers to see if the campaigns are doing what they're supposed to do.

By analyzing things like how many people are buying or clicking on things, businesses can see if their campaigns are convincing people to take action. They can also listen to what customers are saying through surveys or online comments to understand what they like or don't like about the campaigns. This feedback helps them know what they can do better and find ways to make the campaigns more interesting and effective.

Using the data and feedback, businesses can make changes to their campaigns to better match what customers want. They might change the pictures or words they use, or try different ways of telling the story. It's all about learning from the information they have and making choices based on that to make the campaigns more exciting and interesting for the people they want to reach.

In short, by using data and analytics, businesses can see how well their campaigns are doing, learn from customer feedback, and make smart choices to improve their marketing. It's about making sure the campaigns are interesting and appealing to the right people.

Conjuring Compelling Brand Storytelling

In the enchanting realm of marketing, brand storytelling acts as a potent enchantment that enables businesses to set themselves apart from the competition, evoke deep emotions within their audience, and establish meaningful connections with customers. Just like a captivating tale, brand storytelling weaves together elements of imagination, purpose, and authenticity to create a compelling narrative that resonates with people on a profound level.

Through the art of storytelling, business sorcerers can breathe life into their brand, infusing it with a rich tapestry of experiences, values, and aspirations. By crafting a cohesive and engaging story around their brand, they give it depth and substance, making it more than just a product or service. This narrative becomes the guiding force that shapes the brand's identity, positioning it as a character in the ongoing story of its customers' lives.

Brand storytelling is a powerful tool that helps businesses connect with their audience on an emotional level. It allows them to tap into the power of emotions such as joy, curiosity, nostalgia, or even a sense of adventure. By evoking these emotions, the storytelling spell captures the attention and hearts of customers, creating a lasting impression that goes beyond mere advertising or marketing.

Moreover, brand storytelling provides a sense of purpose and meaning to both the business and its customers. By communicating the brand's mission, values, and beliefs through storytelling, businesses establish a deeper connection with their audience. This connection can foster loyalty and advocacy, as customers align themselves with the brand's story and feel a sense of shared values and identity.

In essence, brand storytelling is a magical practice that enables businesses to transcend traditional marketing techniques and create an enchanting experience for their customers. Through the power of storytelling, businesses can captivate their audience, ignite their imagination, and forge lasting connections that go beyond transactions. It is a spell that brings brands to life, infusing them with purpose, meaning, and a touch of magic.

 In the enchanting realm of marketing, brand storytelling acts as a potent enchantment that enables businesses to set themselves apart from the competition, evoke deep emotions within their audience, and establish meaningful connections with customers. Just like a captivating tale, brand storytelling weaves together elements of imagination, purpose, and authenticity to create a compelling narrative that resonates with people on a profound level.

Through the art of storytelling, business sorcerers can breathe life into their brand, infusing it with a rich tapestry of experiences, values, and aspirations. By crafting a cohesive and engaging story around their brand, they give it depth and substance, making it more than just a product or service. This narrative becomes the guiding force that shapes the brand's identity, positioning it as a character in the ongoing story of its customers' lives.

Imagine you're exploring a mystical forest, and you stumble upon a small artisanal chocolate shop. As you enter, you're immediately enchanted by the aroma of rich, high-quality cocoa and the warm, inviting atmosphere. The owner, a passionate chocolatier, greets you with a smile and begins to share the story of their brand.

They tell you about their journey of discovering the finest cacao beans from remote rainforest regions. They describe how each bean is carefully handpicked by local farmers who have cultivated their craft for generations. The chocolatier explains their commitment to sustainability, ensuring fair wages for the farmers and supporting conservation efforts to protect fragile ecosystems.

As they take you on this storytelling journey, you can feel their genuine love and dedication to their craft. They share how their chocolates are meticulously crafted in small batches, using traditional techniques passed down through generations. They describe the passion and artistry that goes into creating each unique flavor combination, from classic dark chocolate to innovative infusions like lavender and sea salt.

Through their brand storytelling, the chocolatier has transformed their small chocolate shop into a magical experience. They've created a narrative that goes beyond simply selling chocolate; it's about connecting with customers on a deeper level. By sharing their story of sustainability, craftsmanship, and commitment to local communities, they've established a sense of authenticity and purpose that resonates with customers.

As you taste their exquisite chocolates, you not only savor the flavors but also feel a sense of connection to the brand. You appreciate the dedication and passion that went into creating these delectable treats. This emotional connection and the story behind the brand make you want to share this enchanting experience with others, becoming an advocate for the chocolatier and their craft.

In this real-life example, the brand storytelling of the artisanal chocolate shop creates a captivating narrative that elevates its products beyond mere confections. By sharing their values, craftsmanship, and commitment to sustainability, they've enchanted customers and forged a meaningful connection that goes beyond a simple transaction. Their brand story has become an integral part of the magical experience they provide, making customers feel like they're part of something special and unique.

 The key to effective brand storytelling lies in authenticity and emotional engagement. Business sorcerers should strive to tell stories that are genuine, and relatable, and evoke emotions such as joy, inspiration, or empathy.

These stories can be shared through various channels, including social media, video content, blog posts, and customer testimonials.

Furthermore, incorporating visual elements such as captivating visuals, videos, and infographics can enhance the storytelling experience and leave a lasting impression on the audience. By weaving a consistent and compelling narrative throughout all touch-points, business sorcerers can create a memorable brand story that resonates with customers and sets them apart from competitors.

Enchanting Customers with Magical Experiences

In the captivating realm of business sorcery, imagine a scenario where a customer walks into a whimsically decorated store. Soft, ambient music fills the air, creating a magical atmosphere. The attentive staff members greet the customers with warm smiles and genuine enthusiasm, instantly making them feel valued and special.

As the customer explores the store, they encounter enchanting displays that showcase products in a visually stunning way. Each item is carefully arranged, accompanied by informative and imaginative descriptions that transport the customer to a world of possibilities. When the customer makes a purchase, they are pleasantly surprised by the seamless and efficient checkout process.

The staff members handle the transaction with grace and efficiency, ensuring that the customer's experience remains magical until the very end. After leaving the store, the customer receives a personalized thank-you email, expressing gratitude for their visit and offering exclusive discounts for future purchases. This thoughtful gesture makes the customer feel appreciated and nurtures a sense of loyalty. Over time, the customer can't help but share their enchanting experience with friends, family, and colleagues. They become an advocate for the store, enthusiastically recommending it to others. Through the power of word-of-mouth marketing, the store's reputation grows, attracting new customers who are eager to experience the magic themselves.

As the relationship between the store and the customer deepens, they find themselves eagerly anticipating new product launches and special events. The store continues to surprise and delight, constantly introducing innovative experiences that keep customers engaged and enthralled.

In this magical business realm, enchanting customers with extraordinary experiences is the key to success. By creating a captivating and memorable journey for every customer, businesses can forge long-lasting relationships, foster customer loyalty, and ultimately thrive in an ever-competitive market. To enchant customers with magical experiences, businesses should prioritize empathy and understanding.

This involves putting themselves in the shoes of their customers and truly comprehending their desires and expectations.

By doing so, they can anticipate the needs of their customers and strive to exceed those expectations at every touchpoint. Personalized interactions play a crucial role in creating magical experiences. The business sorcerers should treat each customer as an individual, tailoring their interactions to suit their preferences and unique requirements. This could involve addressing customers by their names, remembering their previous interactions, and offering personalized recommendations or suggestions. By making customers feel seen and valued, businesses can create a sense of connection and enhance the enchantment of the experience.

Seamless and convenient experiences are also essential in creating magical moments for customers. This means removing any obstacles or complexities that might hinder their journey. Whether it's through streamlined checkout processes, hassle-free returns, and exchanges, or user-friendly digital interfaces, businesses should strive to make every interaction as smooth and effortless as possible. By eliminating friction and making things easy for customers, businesses can enhance the magical aura and leave customers spellbound.

Active listening and responsiveness to customer feedback are vital components of enchanting experiences. By actively seeking and listening to feedback, businesses can gain valuable insights into the needs and desires of their customers. This feedback can be gathered through surveys, social media, or direct conversations with customers.

Taking this feedback to heart and implementing necessary improvements or enhancements demonstrates a commitment to continuously enhancing the magical experience. The willingness to adapt and evolve based on customer input ensures that the enchantment remains fresh and relevant.

Furthermore, businesses can harness the power of technology to craft captivating experiences. With the advent of personalized marketing automation and immersive virtual reality, there are incredible possibilities to engage customers in unique and unforgettable ways. By utilizing these tools strategically, businesses can create enchanting experiences that leave a lasting impression on their customers.

Imagine receiving a personalized email or advertisement that speaks directly to your preferences and interests. Through the use of marketing automation, businesses can analyze customer data and tailor their messages to resonate with individual customers. This level of personalization adds a touch of magic to the customer experience, making customers feel truly understood and valued.

Virtual reality (VR) takes enchantment to a whole new level. Picture stepping into a virtual world where you can explore products or services in a fully immersive and interactive environment. For example, a furniture store could offer a VR experience that allows customers to virtually decorate their homes, trying out different furniture arrangements and styles.

This not only captures customers' imaginations but also provides a practical and engaging way to make purchase decisions. Technology can also enhance convenience and efficiency in the customer journey.

Mobile apps, for instance, allow customers to effortlessly browse products, make purchases, and track their orders on the go. With just a few taps on their smartphones, customers can experience the convenience of seamless transactions and effortless interactions.

Furthermore, technology enables businesses to gather and analyze customer feedback more effectively. Through social media listening tools and sentiment analysis, businesses can gain insights into customer preferences and sentiments, allowing them to refine their strategies and create even more enchanting experiences.

In summary, technology offers businesses an array of tools and opportunities to create enchanting experiences for their customers. From personalized marketing automation to immersive virtual reality, these advancements allow businesses to engage customers in innovative and memorable ways. By leveraging technology strategically and thoughtfully, businesses can weave a layer of digital enchantment into their customer experiences, leaving customers spellbound and eager to return.

Chapter 3: Negotiation Wizardry

In the business world, negotiating is like a powerful tool that helps entrepreneurs shape their deals, make friends, and get good outcomes. This chapter is all about becoming a negotiation wizard. It breaks down the skills and tricks you need to be great at convincing people, using charm and cleverness to turn a "no" into a magical "yes." So, it's like learning the art of business magic to make things go your way.

Mastering the art of persuasion

The art of persuasion is like becoming a negotiation wizard, where the key is to influence others' thoughts and decisions to match your goals. It's a bit like being a smooth talker in the business world, weaving your charm to get what you want. Let's break down the techniques into two:

- **Active Listening Magic:**

Picture this as tuning in to your friend's movie preferences before suggesting your favorite film. In business sorcery, it's crucial to actively listen to the other party's needs, concerns, and perspectives. This isn't just hearing; it's about understanding what makes them tick. By doing this, you can tailor your arguments to resonate with their motivations.

- **Building Rapport and Empathy Spells:**

Think of building rapport and empathy as creating a magical connection, much like bonding with your friend over shared interests. In the business realm, it involves making the other party feel understood and valued. This sense of trust and collaboration is your ticket to a successful negotiation spell.

Now, let's dive into a real-world example: Imagine you're convincing a potential business partner to collaborate on a project. By actively listening to their needs and concerns, you learn that they value innovation and efficiency. You tailor your pitch, emphasizing how your collaboration will bring innovative solutions and streamline processes. As you build rapport by showing understanding and empathy, you create a magical alliance, making them more likely to say "yes" to the partnership.

In essence, mastering persuasion in the realm of negotiation wizardry is about employing these techniques – listening actively and building connections – to cast a spell that aligns others with your objectives. It's not just a communication skill; it's a strategic art that turns conversations into enchanted collaborations.

In the complex world of negotiation wizardry, making a persuasive argument is equivalent to casting a strong spell, with facts and reasoning serving as the magical ingredients.

Consider the following scenario: A business person is proposing a new product to a potential client. They construct a compelling story supported by actual proof by displaying market data, and customer testimonials, and exhibiting the product's distinctive qualities.

Crafting a powerful incantation is similar to communicating a clear and simple value proposition.

Assume the business sorcerer can clearly describe how their product or service matches the client's demands, solves particular difficulties, and offers exceptional advantages. This clarity operates like a charm, drawing the audience's attention and interest.

Anticipating the opposing party's worries and proactively addressing them is part of addressing potential objections. Imagine the sorcerer anticipating inquiries about costs and answering them with details of long-term savings or special discounts for early adoption. It's similar to defending against skepticism ahead of time with prepared answers.

Using storytelling skills is similar to enthralling your audience with a gripping narrative. Imagine the sorcerer telling the story of a

happy client and how the product changed their business.

This story leaves a lasting effect on the audience by ingraining the argument into their mind and making it more sympathetic.

Let's now explore the enchanted world of win-win situations and reciprocity. Imagine that two companies are negotiating about forming a partnership The first business sorcerer proposes a collaboration that not only benefits their company but also offers advantages for the partner. This approach creates a sense of reciprocity, where both parties feel they are gaining value from the agreement.

Seeking win-win solutions involves finding common ground that satisfies the interests of all parties involved. For instance, if negotiating a contract, the sorcerer might identify terms that align with the needs and goals of both sides, ensuring a mutually beneficial outcome. This not only fosters cooperation but also significantly increases the likelihood of reaching a positive agreement.

In essence, mastering the art of persuasion in negotiation wizardry involves skillfully presenting a compelling case, addressing objections, incorporating storytelling, and embracing the principles of reciprocity and win-win solutions. It's a strategic dance where every move is a calculated spell, designed to create an enchanting harmony that leads to successful negotiations in the complex world of business sorcery.

Charm and wit are potent weapons in the negotiation wizard's arsenal. They can disarm opponents, build rapport, and create a positive and collaborative atmosphere. Business sorcerers can employ several strategies to unleash the power of charm and wit in negotiations.

Firstly, maintaining a confident and charismatic demeanor can help establish authority and credibility. Business sorcerers should project confidence in their abilities and radiate positivity, which can be contagious and influence the mood of the negotiation. Using humor strategically can also work wonders. Well-timed jokes or light-hearted anecdotes can diffuse tension, create a sense of camaraderie, and foster a more relaxed and open atmosphere. However, it is essential to use humor judiciously and be mindful of cultural sensitivities.

Active listening and demonstrating genuine interest in the other party's perspective can also enhance charm and rapport building. By showing empathy and understanding, business sorcerers can create a connection that goes beyond the transactional aspects of the negotiation.

Turning No into Yes with Sorceress Skills:

In the realm of negotiation wizardry, turning "no" into "yes" is a coveted skill. It requires finesse, creativity, and a deep understanding of human psychology. Business sorcerers can employ several techniques to achieve this feat.

Firstly, reframing the negotiation and shifting the focus from positions to interests can open up new possibilities. By uncovering the underlying motivations and needs of the other party, business sorcerers can explore alternative solutions that satisfy both parties' interests.

Finding common ground and emphasizing shared objectives can also be effective. Business sorcerers should highlight areas of agreement and align their proposals with the other party's goals. This creates a sense of collaboration and increases the likelihood of a positive outcome.

Moreover, using concessions strategically can be a powerful tool. By offering compromises or sweetening the deal with additional value, business sorcerers can create a sense of reciprocity and a win-win mindset.

Chapter 4: Leading with Enchantment

In the realm of business sorcery, leadership is not just about authority and control but about inspiring and enchanting others to achieve greatness. This chapter explores the principles of leading with enchantment, focusing on how to inspire and motivate your team and create a magical corporate culture.

Inspiring and Motivating Your Team:

To lead with enchantment, business sorcerers must inspire and motivate their teams to reach new heights. Effective leaders understand that motivation goes beyond financial incentives and taps into the intrinsic drivers that fuel passion and commitment. One key aspect of inspiring and motivating a team is setting a compelling vision. Business sorcerers must paint a vivid picture of the future, clearly articulating the mission, values, and goals of the organization. This vision should be inspiring, ambitious, and aligned with the values of the team members.

Furthermore, leaders must lead by example. They should embody the qualities and behaviors they wish to see in their team members, demonstrating integrity, resilience, and a relentless pursuit of excellence. By modeling the desired behaviors, leaders inspire their teams to follow suit and create a culture of high performance.

Effective communication is also essential for inspiring and motivating a team. Business sorcerers must communicate their vision, goals, and expectations clearly and consistently. They should provide regular feedback and recognition to foster a sense of achievement and reinforce positive behaviors. Additionally, creating opportunities for growth and development, such as training programs or challenging assignments, can fuel motivation and engagement.

Creating a Magical Corporate Culture:

A magical corporate culture fosters creativity, collaboration, and a sense of belonging. It is a culture where employees feel inspired, valued, and empowered to contribute their best work. Business sorcerers play a vital role in creating and nurturing such a culture.

First and foremost, a magical corporate culture starts with a strong set of core values. Business sorcerers must define and communicate the values that underpin the organization's identity and guide its actions. These values should be more than mere words on a wall; they should be embedded in the daily practices, decision-making processes, and interactions within the organization.

Creating a culture of trust is also crucial. Business sorcerers should foster an environment where open communication, transparency, and psychological safety are encouraged. Trust allows for collaboration, innovation, and the sharing of ideas and feedback without fear of judgment or reprisal.

Moreover, celebrating diversity and embracing inclusivity is a cornerstone of a magical corporate culture. Business sorcerers should promote a culture that values and respects different perspectives, backgrounds, and experiences. This diversity can fuel innovation and creativity, leading to a more dynamic and resilient organization.

Encouraging and promoting a culture of learning is another essential element. Business sorcerers should encourage continuous learning and provide opportunities for professional growth and development. This can include mentorship programs, training initiatives, or even allocating time for employees to pursue their interests and passions.

Lastly, recognizing and rewarding excellence is vital for creating a magical corporate culture. Business sorcerers should acknowledge and celebrate achievements, both big and small, and create a culture of appreciation and gratitude.

Recognizing and rewarding employees for their contributions not only boosts morale but also reinforces the behaviors and values that drive the organization's success.

In conclusion, leading with enchantment involves inspiring and motivating your team and creating a magical corporate culture. By embracing these principles, business sorcerers can unleash the full potential of their teams, and foster innovation and collaboration.

Chapter 5: The Magic of Customer Experience

The success of any business lies in its ability to create exceptional customer experiences. In Chapter 5, we will explore the magic of customer experience and delve into the strategies that enable businesses to create memorable moments of delight, build customer loyalty and advocacy, and ultimately transform customers into raving fans.

Creating Memorable Moments of Delight

Customers today have high expectations when it comes to their interactions with businesses. It is no longer sufficient to merely meet their needs; businesses must strive to exceed expectations and provide moments of delight that leave a lasting impression. This section will explore the key elements of creating memorable moments of delight, including:

1. Understanding customer needs and desires: By truly understanding your customers' needs, preferences, and desires, you can tailor your products, services, and interactions to exceed their expectations. This requires actively listening to customer feedback, conducting market research, and using data analytics to gain insights into their preferences.

2. Personalization and customization: Customers appreciate personalized experiences that cater to their individual preferences. By leveraging customer data and technology, businesses can create tailored experiences that make customers feel valued and special.

3. Going above and beyond Exceptional customer experiences often stem from going the extra mile. Whether it's providing

unexpected perks, resolving issues promptly and effectively, or surprising customers with unexpected gestures, going above and beyond can turn an ordinary interaction into a memorable one.

Building Customer Loyalty and Advocacy

Loyal customers are the lifeblood of any business. Not only do they generate repeat business, but they also become advocates who spread positive word-of-mouth and attract new customers. In this section, we will explore strategies for building customer loyalty and advocacy, including:

1. Consistency and reliability: Consistency in delivering high-quality products, services, and experiences is crucial for building trust and loyalty. Customers want to know that they can rely on your business to consistently meet their expectations.

2. Building emotional connections: Emotional connections are a powerful driver of customer loyalty. By creating experiences that evoke positive emotions, businesses can forge deeper connections with their customers. This can be achieved through personalized interactions, storytelling, and fostering a sense of community.

3. Rewarding loyalty: Implementing loyalty programs and incentives can incentivize customers to continue doing business with you. By offering exclusive rewards, discounts, and personalized offers, businesses can show their appreciation and encourage repeat purchases.

Transforming Customers into Raving Fans

Raving fans are customers who are not only loyal but also actively promote and advocate for your business. They go beyond being satisfied customers and become ambassadors who willingly share their positive experiences with others. In this section, we will explore strategies to transform customers into raving fans, including:

1. Delighting at every touchpoint: Consistently delivering exceptional experiences at every customer touchpoint is key to creating raving fans. From the first interaction to post-purchase support, each touchpoint is an opportunity to impress and exceed expectations.
2. Encouraging and amplifying positive word-of-mouth: Actively encourage customers to share their positive experiences through reviews, testimonials, and social media. Provide platforms and incentives for customers to share their stories, and amplify their positive feedback to reach a wider audience.
3. Creating a culture of customer-centricity: Transforming customers into raving fans requires a company-wide commitment to customer-centricity.

Conclusion: Unleashing Your Business Magic

As we conclude this transformative journey of business magic, it is time to reflect on the incredible power that lies within every one of us. Throughout this adventure, we have explored the depths of our potential, harnessed the forces of innovation, and discovered the key to unlocking our business magic.

Today, we celebrate the triumphs and challenges that have shaped us into the entrepreneurs and visionaries we are today. We have witnessed the transformational impact of embracing our unique talents, skills, and passions. We have learned that by tapping into our inner reservoirs of creativity and perseverance, we can transcend limits and achieve remarkable success.

The path to business enchantment is not without its hurdles. It requires unwavering commitment, dedication, and a willingness to embrace failure as a stepping stone toward growth. Through the ups and downs, we have learned that true magic lies not just in the achievements, but also in the lessons learned along the way.

As we stand at the precipice of greatness, let us remember that our journey does not end here. We have the power to create a legacy of extraordinary success that will transcend generations. Our businesses have the potential to reshape industries, impact lives, and leave an indelible mark on the world.

Embracing the power within us means recognizing that we are not alone on this path. We have forged valuable connections, built strong networks, and nurtured relationships that will serve as pillars of support and inspiration. Collaboration, mentorship, and the exchange of ideas have proven to be catalysts for unleashing our true potential.

Our business magic extends beyond the confines of profit and growth. It encompasses the transformative impact we have on our employees, customers, and communities. By infusing our businesses with purpose and a commitment to social responsibility, we can create a positive ripple effect that resonates far beyond our immediate sphere of influence.

As we conclude this chapter of our journey, let us carry forward the lessons learned, the triumphs celebrated, and the magic unleashed. Let us continue to push the boundaries of what is possible, challenge the status quo, and embrace the unknown with courage and conviction.
Remember, the power to create, innovate, and enchant lies within you. Embrace your unique strengths, believe in your vision, and never shy away from the audacity of dreaming big. Your business has the potential to be a beacon of light amidst the darkness, a catalyst for change, and a testament to the extraordinary heights that can be reached when we unleash our true potential.
Thank you for joining us on this remarkable journey of business enchantment. May you continue to create magic and leave an indelible mark on the world.

Epilogue: The Never-Ending Quest for Business Magic

As we conclude our exploration of business enchantment, we find ourselves standing at the threshold of a never-ending quest. The pursuit of business magic is not a destination but a lifelong journey of continual learning, evolution, and growth. It is a path that beckons us to explore new realms, challenge our limits, and harness the ever-unfolding power within.

Like skilled sorcerers, we must embrace the notion that mastery is not achieved in a single moment, but through the accumulation of knowledge, experience, and wisdom. The business landscape is ever-changing, and to remain relevant and impactful, we must adapt and evolve with it. We must be open to new ideas, emerging technologies, and shifting paradigms, seeking to understand and harness their potential to create magic in our businesses.

In our pursuit of business magic, we have the power to inspire others to embrace the magic within themselves. By sharing our experiences, insights, and lessons learned, we can ignite the spark of curiosity and passion in aspiring entrepreneurs and future business leaders. We have the opportunity to mentor, guide, and empower those around us, nurturing a community of innovative thinkers who will continue to push the boundaries of what is possible.

But the true measure of our quest lies not only in personal growth or individual success. It is in the lasting impact we leave on the world of business. Just as a sorcerer's legacy is determined by the mark they leave on the magical realm, our legacy is defined by the positive change we bring to our industries, our communities, and the lives of those we touch.

As business sorcerers, we can create organizations that prioritize purpose, sustainability, and social responsibility. We can build companies that not only generate profits but also contribute to the greater good. By infusing our businesses with a sense of purpose and aligning them with the values we hold dear, we can leave a lasting impact that transcends the boundaries of time. In this never-ending quest for business magic, let us not forget the importance of embracing the journey itself.

The challenges we face, the lessons we learn, and the connections we forge along the way are all part of the enchanting tapestry of entrepreneurship. It is through these experiences that we grow, evolve, and become the sorcerers we are meant to be.
As we close this chapter, let us carry forward the spirit of curiosity, the thirst for knowledge, and the unwavering belief in the magic that lies within us. May our pursuit of business enchantment be a beacon of inspiration for others, illuminating the path to greatness and igniting the flames of possibility.
The quest for business magic is a never-ending adventure, an eternal dance with the forces of innovation, resilience, and creativity. Embrace this quest with an open heart and a steadfast spirit, and may your journey be filled with wonder, discovery, and the realization of extraordinary dreams.